Navigating

Educational

Turbulence

How to Land the Plane

Dr. Michael Triplett

ISBN- 979-8-218—35683-5
Printed and bound in the United States of America
First Printing 2024
Editing by Kimberli Wilson, Let's Book Up Professional
Editing Services
Book Cover Design by Raygan Clark
Interior Formatting by: Sierra Dean, Dean Diaries Publishing

To order additional copies of this book, contact the author:
miketrip1992@gmail.com
https://doctripthegamechanger.com/

Dedication

I dedicate this book to the educational leaders who demonstrate a genuine interest and compassion for educating our children. They commit themselves with understanding that there will be nuances that must be navigated in an effort to support faculty and staff who educate and make a difference in the lives of all students they support.

To them: You are willing to take on the challenge of teaching children and supporting staff who enter our districts each day, prepared or unprepared to teach and learn. There are obstacles placed in your way, making it difficult for you to perform day in and day out, yet you never give up.

For the most part, my book is dedicated to our children. We know that whether you attend school in urban, rural or suburban school districts, there are educational distinctions that we as leaders must navigate in order to provide you with the most amazing educational experiences imaginable.

Finally, I want to dedicate this book to my entire family Turner/Hendricks, friends, and those 89 blocks of East St. Louis, Illinois.

Special thanks my editor—Kimberli J. Wilson, Chief Editor of Let's Book Up!

Foreword

We can learn a great deal from observing others. When a leader makes entry into an organization and greets everyone with a calm spirit, humble conversation and a focused mindset, it speaks volumes about the charisma of that leader. The audience becomes intrigued by the person and wants to be enlightened by spending even more time around that leader. Leadership is inclusive of influence, ability to inspire, forge relationships, decision making and collaboration. These skills are at the forefront of safeguarding a positive organizational climate and culture. As a result, it is also difficult to master the craft within a specified parameter of time. It is rather, a lifetime commitment to the mastery of leadership itself. The leader who remains calm during the storm and humble whether things are going wrong or right, maintains the stewardship of those for whom he or she provides both supervision and empowerment.

While navigating the obstacles often encountered in education, we are repeatedly faced with human conflict, district-level vs. building-level philosophies, community issues, student achievement and test scores, discipline outcomes and parent concerns. As a leader you are trained and expected to swiftly navigate through the turbulence and resolve challenges in an equitable manner. The decision-making process should reflect state requirements, district philosophy, the supervisor's vision, parents' concerns, and also student achievement expectations. The reflection of each area is often a skill-set established by seeking observation opportunities from a mentor and guided conversations. Mistakes are natural outcomes as leaders navigate the obstacles of education. Integral to the development, growth and success of a great leader, is the formulation of a relationship with a mentor to embark on the journey of educational leadership. The pathway to success, including the occasional failure, is most often journeyed easier when the leader has been mentored appropriately, remains a calm and assuring presence, is knowledgeable, focused and leads with both confidence and humility.

Dr. Michael Triplett has a calm demeanor, humble yet commanding presence and a focused mindset for leading and guiding others through the turbulence that educational leadership brings. He consistently listens to the voices of others for the opportunity to impact an equitable solution. He provides mentees with opportunities for growth with positive choices and alternative outcomes. As a leader/mentor, he continues to guide my footsteps in the correct direction with encouragement, redirection and innovative freedom to be successful. In his book "Navigating Educational Turbulence - How to Land the Plane," he shares specific strategies for new and seasoned leaders to implement for successful outcomes. The daily practices are the foundational success factors for weekly, monthly and yearly growth to guiding others. I continue to use Dr. Triplett's book as a road map for leadership growth and success and I encourage others to do the same.

Table of Contents

BEGIN HERE....

Educational Leaders frequently enter their positions with great expectations of having a significant impact on their schools and communities. But in practice, being an educational leader, whether at the district or school level, as a department chair, a PLC leader, or a leader at the grade level, can be difficult and turbulent. Many discover that they are unprepared for the complexity and nuances of the job. Good leadership in education necessitates not just a thorough understanding of how people learn but also the capacity to unite people and give each member of their team a voice. As a result, it is necessary for universities and feeder programs, as well as experienced leaders, to inform aspiring leaders about the challenges and advantages of being an Educational Leader.

Not having a complete understanding of the many different cultures that make up the varying communities they serve is one of the major obstacles facing educational leaders. Accepting communities are less likely to be receptive to in-coming leaders because the historical needs of both groups are different. Consequently, a deeper understanding of the community's distinct dynamics, culture and ambitions are essential to navigating this gap.

The objective is to create a shared vision that takes everyone's needs into account. A leader must have meaningful conversations with stakeholders, including parents, teachers, students, and community members in order to achieve this goal.

The varied disturbances and difficulties that educators face together are referred to as educational turbulence. Changes in regulations and curricula, as well as shifts in student demographics and societal expectations, are just a few of the numerous ways that these turbulences might appear. Leaders must possess the ability to recognize these subtle differences as well as the willingness to pivot and adjust their strategies to guarantee the school stays on course, despite outside challenges.

A Changing Population and a Range of Needs

The classroom environment is heavily impacted by the demographic changes that schools experience frequently. Language hurdles, a range of learning styles, and cultural variations are just a few of the particular difficulties that come with a diverse student body. In an effort to guarantee that every student receives an equitable education, embracing inclusivity and establishing a culture that promotes variety; becomes essential for administrators.

Economic and Social Pressures

External socio-economic elements that have an impact on a kids' life outside of school further exacerbates the already turbulent educational climate. The effects of poverty, homelessness, and other societal issues on the wellbeing and academic performance of their students must be taken into account by leaders. Helping students overcome these challenges and achieve academic success depends on their involvement with local resources and support networks.

Curriculum and Policy Changes

Leaders must manage the constantly shifting terrain of curricular requirements and educational regulations. State and federal educational standards are frequently revised, necessitating flexibility and a readiness to accept cutting-edge teaching techniques. However, leaders must balance following these rules along with modification to meet the unique requirements of their students and community.

A combination of strong leadership abilities, fortitude, and a dedication to continual development are needed to navigate the educational turmoil. Here are some techniques that can help school administrators overcome obstacles and excel in their positions:

1. Develop a Common Vision:

Stakeholders can be brought together and given a sense of purpose through a compelling and clear vision for the school. Leaders may foster a collective commitment to accomplishing shared objectives by including every member of the school community in the visioning process.

2. Collaborative decision-making is encouraged:

Making decisions in a collaborative manner with feedback from staff, students, and community members is a key component of effective leadership. This strategy not only ensures that many viewpoints are taken into account, but it also fosters a culture of trust and empowerment.

3. Develop Professionally to Grow Capacity:

Teachers and staff must make an investment in professional development if they are to increase their ability to meet the changing requirements of children. Leaders must pinpoint the precise areas in which their team needs assistance and then deliver specialized training and resources in accordance.

4. Encourage a positive school climate:

The basis for success is an environment at school that is supportive and diverse. In order to foster a culture where everyone feels appreciated, encouraged, and inspired to succeed, school leaders must place a high priority on the health and well-being of their faculty and students.

5. Participate in External Partnerships

Building solid relationships with local businesses, groups, and leaders can give the school access to important resources and support. Addressing societal issues that can have an impact on students' academic achievement can be accomplished by working with outside partners.

Education turbulence is an unavoidable part of school leadership, but with the appropriate approaches and outlook, administrators can steer their institutions through difficulties and toward success. When educational leaders are apprised of particular requirements of their communities, ways to promote diversity, and the methods for developing a common vision, they are properly prepared to create an environment where both students and teachers will thrive.

It is pressing that we equip the upcoming generation of educational leaders with the skills and knowledge necessary to face turbulence head-on and turn it into an opportunity for growth and constructive change. School leaders can achieve their goals of having a long-lasting and significant impact on education by being dedicated, flexible, and committed to serving their communities.

CHAPTER 1

The development of young minds, the promotion of knowledge expansion, and the stimulation of research and creativity are all facilitated by educational leaders, notably school principals. With their persistent commitment to teaching, research, and service, they serve as the foundation of the educational system. A school principal's journey is however, anything but simple; it is one that is fraught with difficulties and upheavals that tests their resiliency and dedication.

➤ Navigating the Academic Job Market and Tenure Track Pressures:

The demanding academic job market presents a substantial obstacle for future educational leaders. Outstanding research ability, teaching talent, and strong networking abilities are required to land a tenure-track position at a top school. Many highly competent candidates lack solid career possibilities as a result of the dearth of tenure-track positions, which intensifies competitiveness.

Once in their jobs, teachers and principals must meet the requirements of the tenure track. For tenure, they must exhibit a strong research portfolio, perform exceptionally in teaching evaluations, and make a major contribution to the expansion of the school. The prolonged tenure evaluation process, which frequently lasts for several years, introduces high levels of stress that can have an adverse effect on one's mental health and professional performance.

➤ Balancing Teaching and Research Demands:

Finding a balance between the demands of teaching and research is one of the biggest issues that leadership faces. While they need to create a welcoming learning environment, encourage student interaction, and provide compelling lectures; in order to develop their academic careers, they must continue to pursue an active research agenda, publish papers in prestigious journals, and obtain research funding.

Burnout can be caused by the constant juggling of teaching and research responsibilities, which compromises educational quality and academic development. It is urgent to achieve balance between these key elements, yet doing so is frequently difficult because of time restrictions and conflicting demands.

➢ Confronting the "Publish or Perish" Culture:

School principals are under a lot of pressure to constantly deliver research findings because of the pervasive "publish or perish" mentality. The amount and quality of publications are important factors in grant approval, promotions, and tenure. While aiming for high-impact articles is admirable, doing so can take a lot of time and effort and may prevent researchers from exploring novel yet transformational research directions.

Moreover, the pressure to publish frequently may degrade study quality, producing results that are insufficient or erroneous. The emphasis on formal publication in this culture can make it more difficult for researchers to cooperate and share their knowledge.

➢ Navigating Funding and Resource Constraints:

The inability of school administrators to secure research funds prevents the completion of ambitious investigations. Researcher potential is hampered by a lack of funding opportunities and intense competition. Budgetary constraints impede academic research and thereby limits the ability to access essential databases, tools, and resources.

Limited resources also affect educational settings, which show up as increased class sizes, dated infrastructure, and insufficient funding for instructional materials. Effective teaching strategies are compromised by these limitations, which also harm students' overall educational experiences.

➤ Addressing Diverse Learning Needs and Student Engagement:

For school administrators, creating a welcoming and engaging learning environment is a significant issue. They must accommodate students with a range of learning needs, abilities, and motivations. It is often challenging to strike a balance between providing personalized instruction and maintaining academic standards.

The rapid advancement of technology also creates both opportunities and difficulties. Although incorporating technology can improve learning, doing so involves continual modifications and may pose a gap between students and teachers who are accustomed to conventional teaching techniques.

13

➤ Balancing Work-Life and Prioritizing Mental Health:

Given the blending of personal and professional lives, superintendents continue to struggle with maintaining a healthy work-life balance. Stress, burnout, and other mental health issues can be made worse by long workdays, weekend commitments, and relentless performance demands.

These difficulties are exacerbated by inadequate institutional support for mental health, which forces school leaders to deal with problems largely on their own. The stigma around mental health in the educational community makes it harder for people to ask for and accept help.

➤ Maneuvering Institutional Politics and Bureaucracy:

Another challenge is navigating the political dynamics and administrative red tape that exists inside educational institutions. Power struggles, prejudices, and competing interests can create a poisonous workplace environment that lowers school principals' morale and productivity.

The introduction of revolutionary changes, the distribution of resources, and the implementation of initiatives can all be hampered by bureaucratic red tape. It is a constant struggle to navigate problematic issues while respecting morals and academic standards.

➤ Embracing Technological Advancements and Overcoming Skills Gap

School administrators realize that the quick development of technology presents both benefits and challenges. Learning and research outcomes can be improved by utilizing digital technologies and cutting-edge teaching techniques. However, reluctance to change may prevent adaptation, leaving a skills deficit in the field of education.

15

In an effort to stay abreast with shifting pedagogical paradigms and technological trends, school leaders must actively participate in continual learning and professional development.

➢ Overestimating Institutional Support

I've learned the value of being watchful about potential blind spots that may divert my route and reduce my effectiveness as a school principal throughout the course of my career. The belief that my university or any other institution would offer all the support I need for a successful academic career was a key blind spot. I've discovered that self-advocacy and initiative are equally important in successfully navigating the challenges and uncertainties that come with scholastic turbulence. Nonetheless, institutions unquestionably play a major role in promoting academic achievement.

I fully believe in developing a growth mindset and being open to criticism as a school principal. Actively seeking out chances for ongoing professional development, whether through workshops, conferences, or other venues, is needed. Using this strategy has helped me find and address blind spots I might have otherwise missed, thus improving my leadership and decision-making capabilities.

Intentionally keeping the lines of communication open with my peers, mentors, and students, has broadened my perspective and I've become more self-aware. Finding new angles and having deep conversations help me identify areas of opportunity that might have an effect on my work as a principal of a school. Each interaction provided insightful information that contributes to making decisions that are in the best interest of the students and the entire school community.

I've discovered that creating a collaborative environment inside the classroom setting is a powerful technique to eliminate blind spots and encourage ongoing development. By fostering open communication, idea sharing, and teamwork, we create an environment that encourages everyone to play to their strengths and fix their collective deficiencies. This approach has not only resulted in creative ideas, but it has also kept me on track and prevented deviations.

Building a strong and diverse intellectual network has been extremely helpful in my work as a school principal. Making connections with other educators, going to conferences, and joining organizations for professionals has provided access to a variety of viewpoints and thoughts. This network consists of a dependable forum for exchanging ideas, discussion about confronting problems and developing a more thorough grasp of any potential areas of weakness that might affect my leadership.

School principals face a variety of difficulties on their path. For the purpose of creating a welcoming climate that supports educators' pursuit of excellence and knowledge, these issues must be acknowledged and addressed. Success is reliant upon resiliency, adaptability, and a passion for learning and study.

School administrators can successfully traverse the challenges of educational upheaval by adopting growth mindsets, asking for feedback, and building a network of peers and mentors. This will have a long-lasting effect on their professional lives as well as the students they lead.

CHAPTER 2

Turbulence has become a frequent occurrence in the dynamic world of education. Turbulence can take many different forms, including cultural transitions, economic fluctuations, legislative changes, technology breakthroughs, and educational innovations.

In order for institutions, faculties, and students to be guided toward success, educational leaders must be aware of and comprehend each type of turbulence. This chapter explores the significance of developing turbulence-navigation skills in the classroom and emphasizes the vital role that leadership plays in meeting these issues.

Technological Uncertainty: New learning opportunities are being created by technological advancements, which are upending conventional teaching strategies and changing the face of education. In order to remain current and give students the skills they need for the job market of the future, leaders must embrace technology and incorporate it into the educational process.

1. Understanding Turbulence in Education:

Policy Uncertainty: Educational policies and rules are subject to quick changes that may have an effect on curricula, funding, and assessment procedures. Leaders must stay abreast of policy amendments, modify their approaches accordingly, and promote legislation that advances the objectives of the organization.

Economic Uncertainty: Funding fluctuations, financial limitations, and economic uncertainties can provide serious difficulties for educational institutions. Leaders need to focus investments in areas that improve educational quality, practice responsible financial management, and research alternate sources of funding.

Social Uncertainty: Cultural and societal changes can have an impact on student behavior, expectations, and learning preferences. Leaders must create a welcoming climate that caters to many needs and equips pupils to succeed in a heterogeneous society.

Pedagogical Uncertainty: Innovative techniques to learning and teaching are constantly being developed. Leaders should support educators' professional growth so that they can adopt cutting-edge pedagogies and provide memorable educational experiences.

2. The Importance of Navigating Turbulence in Education:

Learning how to navigate turbulence in education is critical for several reasons:

1. *Student Success:* Disruptions to the learning process can have a negative effect on students' performance. Despite the difficulties, strong leadership ensures that kids receive a consistent, high-quality education. Education institutions must be robust if they are to survive in a volatile climate. Effective leadership can promote

flexibility, which will help organizations face change head-on and come out stronger.

2. *Relevance and Competitiveness*: Institutions can maintain their relevance and competitiveness while navigating instability. Leaders who embrace innovation and change, places their organizations on the cutting edge of educational success.

3. *Sustainability*: Unpredictability can result in institutional instability and even collapse. Effective leadership handles financial and organizational concerns which results in sustainability.

4. *Employee Confidence and Commitment*: Staff confidence, morale, and devotion to the institution's mission are all boosted by leadership that successfully navigates turmoil.

3. The Role of Leadership in Navigating Turbulence:

Educational institutions need strong leadership to get them through difficult times. In this situation, a few essential leadership qualities are important:

1. *Strategic planning and vision*: A visionary leader, establishes a clear course and creates a strategy that aligns with the values and objectives of the organization. This plan needs to include alternate courses of action in the event of turbulence. Leaders must welcome change and view turbulence as a chance for development and advancement. They must cultivate a culture that respects innovation and ongoing development.

2. *Communication and Transparency*: In turbulent times, open communication is essential. In order to promote a sense of trust and cooperation, leaders must keep all stakeholders up to date on issues, plans, and developments.

3. *Collaborative Decision-Making*: Including a variety of stakeholders in the decision-making process, such as faculty, staff, students, and the community, improves the efficacy of the solutions put into place.

4. *Resilience and Adaptability*: Leaders should provide an example of both traits, encouraging followers to face challenges head-on and with courage.

Educators and employees that feel empowered are more likely to be proactive in resolving problems and looking for possibilities during difficult times. Leaders should support teachers and staff and promote professional development.

Risk management requires leaders to recognize possible hazards and create mitigation plans. Risk management done proactively can avert disasters and lessen their effects.

The success, sustainability, and expansion of educational institutions depend on their capacity to navigate turbulence in the field of education. Understanding and developing successful tactics to meet difficulties head-on are high-priority leadership skills. Leaders may steer their institutions through these trying times by; 1) embracing change, 2) encouraging resilience, 3) fostering collaboration, 4) empowering stakeholders, and 5) emerging stronger and more relevant in the fast-paced world of education. Educational Leaders are more influential in students' lives and help to create a brighter future for generations through creative leadership.

CHAPTER 3

The difficulties of preserving a strong culture and environment within a school community can frequently resemble sailing through choppy waters for an educational leader. The interaction between culture and climate has a significant impact on how both students and staff learn overall. In this chapter, we'll explore seven major areas of concern and practical solutions for dealing with them, including how to set or change the climate when the culture is off, manage diverse personalities, reach a balance between mandates and filters, offer targeted professional development, encourage staff alignment, provide social and emotional support, and lead with empathy and sympathy.

1. *Setting or Re-Setting the Culture Climate*

The culture of a school determines how people interact, form relationships, and feel about themselves. However, educational leaders are obligated to start a climate reset when the culture strays off course. Start by determining the underlying reasons for cultural mismatch through surveys, focus groups, and open discussions. Involve stakeholders in frank discussion to learn about their viewpoints and worries. Develop practical solutions to the problems, such as specialized training, workshops, and community-building initiatives. It's crucial to promote principles like respect, inclusivity, and collaboration while also serving as an example of the desired cultural shifts. Employ a method of tracking progress and frequently recognizing accomplishments as a means of maintaining excitement.

2. *Managing Different Personalities*

A diverse workforce offers a richness of viewpoints to the school community, but it can also present problems for collaboration and cohesiveness. Embrace each person's individuality while encouraging a group commitment to the vision and objectives of the institution. Adopt a solution-oriented approach for resolving disagreements and misconceptions as soon as they arise, create clear communication channels and promote open discussion. Conduct team-building activities that emphasize cooperation and strengths so that employees may respect one another's contributions.

The power of synthesizing various personalities to establish a more robust and coherent school culture encourages an atmosphere of respect and understanding among all members of the school community.

3. Balancing Mandates and Filtering Systems

It can be difficult for educational leaders to connect policies with practices while maintaining the distinctive character of their institution. The goal is to create a solid filtering system that includes mandates that meet the aims and values of the institution, as well as emphasize regulations that support the mission of the school and the academic performance of the students. Openly discuss decision justifications with your workers, and whenever possible; involve them in the decision-making process. Strive to reach balance between conformity and creativity, using regulations as catalysts for expansion rather than limitations.

4. Providing Targeted Professional Development

The key to equipping teachers with the abilities and information they require to effectively support diverse learners is differentiated professional development. With ongoing evaluation and criticism, teachers can identify their strengths and areas of competence. Individualize professional development possibilities by mixing workshops, seminars, peer mentorship, and internet resources. Praising and honoring teachers' accomplishments and development promotes a culture of lifelong learning. Making an investment in individualized professional development provides your staff with the needed tools to provide students with training that caters to their various needs.

5. Fostering Alignment Among Staff

It takes deliberate effort to keep staff members on the same page, especially when they are dispersed among various locations or departments. Regular communication is needed to ensure that everyone is on the same page with regards to goals, priorities, and projects. Use online forums, newsletters, and scheduled gatherings to communicate updates and recognize accomplishments. Establish cross-functional teams so that employees may collaborate on projects while exchanging ideas and viewpoints from multiple angles. You may improve the school community's overall performance by developing a feeling of shared responsibility.

6. Promoting Social and Emotional Support

Prioritizing the social and emotional well-being of both staff and students is essential in the ever-evolving educational environment. Establish a comprehensive support system that includes resources for managing stress and burnout, wellness initiatives, and counseling services. In effort to minimize stigma and establish a comfortable environment for seeking assistance, promote open dialogue about mental health. As a leader in education, exhibit self-care behaviors while stressing the value of work-life balance and stress reduction. You can foster an environment where employees and kids may flourish by putting a high priority on social and emotional support.

7. Leading with Empathy and Sympathy

Effective educational leadership is based on achieving a balance between the heart and the brain. Empathy needs the capacity to fully know and relate to the experiences of others, whereas sympathy entails understanding and offering support based on similar feelings. Engage in conversations that demonstrate sincere concern for others well-being by practicing active listening. Celebrate achievements and landmarks and lend a sympathetic ear to those going through difficult times. Leading with empathy and sympathy will show your team that you value their efforts and are concerned about their personal and professional development.

As an educational leader, you must take a comprehensive approach that blends strategic decision-making with an in-depth knowledge of human dynamics to navigate the turbulence around culture and climate. You can create a school environment where both staff and students thrive by establishing or changing the climate, managing multiple personalities, balancing mandates, offering targeted professional development, fostering alignment, encouraging social and emotional support, and leading with empathy and sympathy. Remember that while the trip may be difficult, you can direct your school community toward a better and more peaceful future with perseverance and the appropriate tactics.

CHAPTER 4

Your responsibilities as an educational leader go far beyond those of conventional management. The difficulties and obstacles you experience in today's dynamic and constantly changing educational environment are comparable to navigating through wild seas. This chapter explores the field of Systems Thinking, a potent strategy that gives you the abilities to not only weather these storms but also guide your educational institution into a more promising future. We will look at six key tactics, each of which addresses a problem that educational leadership faces.

1) Proactive vs. Reactive: Anticipating the Ripples

Pain Point: Reactive leadership perpetuates a cycle of continual crisis management, draining resources and stifling growth.

Responding to problems as they arise is comparable to trying to patch holes in a ship that is already sinking. On the other hand, being proactive entails seeing the waves before they become ripples. Conventional leadership frequently commits the error of firefighting, concentrating on current problems without taking into account the underlying processes behind them. By embracing systems thinking, you may prevent recurring issues and promote a culture of sustainable progress; this is the ability to recognize and solve root causes.

2) Understanding How Your Space Operates: Peering into the Educational Ecosystem

Pain Point: Ignorance of the system's dynamics leads to disjointed efforts, misalignment, and unintended consequences.

You need a deep understanding of the complex web of connections and interdependencies inside your educational ecosystem to lead effectively. You are urged by systems thinking, to look at the broad picture and discover how various elements interact and have an impact on one another. This knowledge not only makes hidden patterns visible, but also aids in making wise decisions.

3) Driving the Team Approach: Orchestrating Collaborative Symphony

Pain Point: A top-down leadership style stifles innovation, alienates stakeholders, and limits the potential for holistic solutions.

The age of the lone leader making decrees on their own has passed. Soliciting the help of your academic staff, stakeholders' varied viewpoints and collective wisdom along with Systems Thinking-- places a strong emphasis on the team approach. You can gain access to a variety of knowledge and increase team members' sense of ownership and commitment by encouraging a collaborative environment.

4) Moving Away from Individuality: Cultivating a Shared Vision

Pain Point: A culture of individualism breeds competition, erodes collaboration, and hampers the institution's ability to adapt and thrive.

Each and every decision in a system has a cascading influence on the whole. You can coordinate your efforts to achieve joint objectives by shifting your attention from individual accomplishments to a shared vision. By encouraging collaboration and interdependence, Systems Thinking helps all stakeholders feel a sense of belonging and oneness.

5) Protocols and Procedures: Synchronizing the Movements

Pain Point: Lack of standardized protocols results in chaos, inconsistencies, and a perpetual reinvention of the wheel.

Systems that work effectively must follow established protocols and processes. They act as the compass points that guarantee efficient operations and reliable results. When your educational institution's demands change, embracing Systems Thinking encourages you to critically evaluate your current protocols, make adjustments based on real-time feedback, and continually enhance them.

6) *Creating Your Playbook: Operationalizing Your Space*

Pain Point: Absence of a systematic approach results in ad-hoc decision-making, missed opportunities for growth, and an inability to navigate turbulent waters.

Systems Thinking is not only a theoretical idea; it is also a set of useful tools that can be put to use to effect real change. You may use it as a reference guide to overcome the challenges of educational leadership, provide methods for analyzing complicated problems, an illustration of causal chains, and creating treatments that result in long-lasting changes. Your leadership is flexible and effective because your playbook changes along with your institution.

Problem Solving emerges as a guiding light in the stormy sea of educational leadership, revealing a route to proactive, all-encompassing, and effective leadership. Understanding the problems mentioned in this chapter and adopting the Systems Thinking principles will enable you to face the difficulties head-on and build a strong educational institution that adapts well to change. Keep in mind that Systems Thinking's real power lies not just in its theoretical elegance but also in its demonstrable capacity to change educational leadership from reactive to visionary, from isolated to collaborative, and from uncertain to empowered.

CHAPTER 5

Every school administrator must manage a few constants in the ever -changing world of educational leadership. The difficult terrain of management and supervision is explored in this chapter, illuminating the key elements that educational leaders must grasp to guide their institutions toward success.

Section 1: The Importance of Time Management

Effective time management is imperative for a school principal since time is the most valuable resource for educators. Leaders must juggle administrative duties, teacher support, student engagement, and personal obligations. As a result, they frequently feel overburdened. Here, we look at methods for enhancing time management and keeping a positive work-life balance:

1.1 Prioritizing Tasks

Leaders in education must distinguish between urgent and significant responsibilities. Prioritizing tasks reduces the chance of burnout while ensuring that urgent issues are handled quickly. A useful tool for making decisions is the Eisenhower Matrix, which divides tasks into four quadrants: urgent and important, not urgent but important, urgent but not important, and neither urgent nor important.

1.2 Delegation and Empowerment

Task delegation promotes employee empowerment and a sense of ownership. Principals might concentrate on high-impact initiatives by giving specific tasks to capable team members. The principal's burden is reduced by giving teachers and staff more autonomy, and the school community is also encouraged to pursue professional development.

1.3 Time-Blocking and Calendar Management

Time-blocking tactics are used by educational leaders to set aside particular times for different tasks. Setting aside time for certain activities improves focus and minimizes distractions, whether it's for staff meetings, or personal rejuvenation.

1.4 Reflecting and Adapting

Principals can improve their methods by periodically assessing their time management techniques. Reflection on successes and failures helps identify what is working and what needs to be changed, enabling continual progress.

Section 2: Managing the Money

The management of finances falls to school principals as custodians of tax payer money. Sound financial management confirms that funds are allocated wisely to improve educational outcomes and uphold transparency:

2.1 Budgeting and Resource Allocation

It is vital to develop a budget that is organized efficiently and supports the objectives of the school. Principals should involve important parties in the budgeting process and verify that a portion of money is reserved to support projects for teaching and learning, professional growth, and facility upgrades.

2.2 Grant Acquisition

Grant applications can be used to complement the school budget and make it possible to undertake creative initiatives. Principals can do some fact-finding for opportunities and work with teachers to locate initiatives that meet grant criteria.

2.3 Data-Informed Decision Making

Principals can make wise decisions by analyzing financial data. Leaders can spot areas for improvement and make changes accordingly by monitoring spending trends, student results, and resource usage.

2.4 Transparent Communication

Fostering trust and accountability within the school community requires honest communication regarding the institution's financial situation. Principals should communicate information on a frequent basis with staff, parents, and students to ensure that everyone is aware of resource allocation and budgetary decisions.

Section 3: Work-Life Balance

It is a constant struggle to maintain a balance between personal well-being and the duties of being a school principal. Nonetheless, for ongoing performance and to avoid burnout; work-life balance is essential:

3.1 Setting Boundaries

It is imperative to establish clear lines of demarcation between business and personal life. In order to encourage staff to adopt similar behaviors, principals should explain these boundaries to their teams and set a good example for them.

3.2 Self-Care and Wellness

Setting self-care as a priority has advantages for the person as well as for the school community. By participating in activities that support students' overall wellness—physical, emotional, and mental—principals can help create a culture of wellness at their institution.

3.3 Delegating Responsibility

The principle is able to take a backseat when necessary by giving assistant principals and other team members the authority to assume leadership positions. A single point of failure is avoided, and professional development is facilitated by delegation of responsibility.

3.4 Flexibility and Adaptability

Unexpected difficulties will inevitably develop because the educational world is dynamic. In order to deal with uncertainty and maintain a healthy balance in their lives, teachers must develop flexibility and resilience.

Section 4: Surviving When You Know the Calvary is Not Coming

Being in a leadership position in education can occasionally feel lonely, especially when faced with difficulties that appear insurmountable. This section discusses how principals can lead their schools through adversity and through challenging circumstances:

4.1 Resourceful Problem-Solving

Principals must use their creativity when outside resources are scarce. Innovative solutions can result from creative problem-solving, working with community partners, and utilizing available resources.

4.2 Building Resilient Teams

Teams should foster a culture of resilience under the direction of their principals. The ability of a team to overcome challenges is influenced by encouraging a growth attitude, offering continual professional development, and rewarding achievements.

4.3 Seeking Peer Support

Participating in peer networks, both physically and digitally, allows principals to exchange experiences, get suggestions, and learn from those who have dealt with similar problems.

4.4 Communicating Hope and Vision

Principals must present a compelling future vision, even in the face of hardship. Galvanizing efforts and fostering change can be accomplished by instilling hope and uniting the school community around a common goal.

Section 5: Navigating the Politics

Navigating a complicated web of political factors is frequently a need of educational leadership. This section explores techniques that principals can use to efficiently handle and juggle the complex realm of educational politics:

5.1 Stakeholder Engagement

It is essential to establish trusting connections with all parties involved, including teachers, parents, and members of the school board. In order to establish alignment and get support for the school's efforts, principals should actively engage these groups.

5.2 Communicating Transparently

Principals can avoid political snares by communicating openly and honestly with one another. Misunderstandings are reduced by keeping stakeholders informed about decisions, justification, and possible effects.

5.3 Focusing on the Mission

Notwithstanding political constraints, maintaining a commitment to the school's goal and vision acts as a compass. The best course of action for students and the larger educational community should be the guiding factors for a principal's decisions.

5.4 Advocacy and Leadership

At higher levels of governance, principals should speak up for the needs of their school. They may magnify their voice and have an impact on policy by working with district officials and community partners.

A diverse approach to management and supervision is necessary given the tumultuous environment of educational leadership. School administrators need to be adept in time management, money management, work-life balance, being resilient in the face of difficulties, and navigating the complexities of educational politics. Educational leaders can guide their institutions toward success while establishing a vibrant school community that places a priority on the development and well-being of students by implementing these tactics.

Chapter 6

Harnessing Partnerships, Fostering Collaborative Spirit, and Boosting Team Productivity

"Alone we can do so little; together we can achieve so much."
- Helen Keller

Educational leadership operates in an ever-evolving educational landscape. Navigating educational turbulence surrounding the formation of productive teams is a significant challenge. In this comprehensive exploration, we delve deeply into the problems that lead to conflicts and examine effective methods for fostering a positive, influential, and highly productive team environment. As Helen Keller once wisely stated, "Alone we can do so little; together we can achieve so much."

1. Partnerships as a Catalyst for Positive Outcomes

Education institutions are becoming more and more aware of how effective collaboration can be in achieving successful results. In an interconnected world, forming alliances among stakeholders from many fields of expertise can have a revolutionary impact. This voyage is not without its difficulties, though.

Turbulence Point 1: Navigating the Partnership Landscape

Navigating the partnership landscape is one of the main pain areas. It might be difficult to find the right partners, set clear goals, and ensure mutual gain. Goal misalignment, poor communication, and power dynamics can result in conflict and stagnation.

Navigational Strategies:

a) *Shared vision and goal setting*: This should be established first. All stakeholders are brought together by this fundamental stage, which also establishes a shared direction.

b) *Open Communication Channels*: Provide frequent communication channels to promote openness and understanding among people. Frequent check-ins and updates on the status of the project might reduce misconceptions.

c) *Redistribution of Power*: Recognize and address power relationships in partnerships. Promote an equitable allocation of power so that every voice is heard and respected.

2) The Triumph of "We" over "I" and "Me"

The key to a successful educational venture is collaboration. However, individualism and ego can cause turbulence and impede the advancement of a cohesive team.

Turbulence Point 2: Individualism vs. Team Cohesion

It is a constant struggle to strike a balance between team members' individual aims and the organization's overall objectives. Teams may become disjointed, there may be conflicting agendas, and results may be jeopardized when the "I" and the "Me" take precedence over the "We".

Harmony-Driven Strategies:

a) *Create a Culture of Collaboration:* Encourage a society where teamwork is valued and embraced. Draw attention to examples of effective teamwork and the benefits it brings to the educational sector.

b) *Value Diversity:* Stress the importance of many viewpoints. Encourage team members to recognize the value that individuals with diverse experiences and points of view may contribute.

c) *Shared Accountability:* Encourage a sense of shared accountability and responsibility. When team members take responsibility for both their triumphs and mistakes, the focus shifts from individual recognition to group accomplishment.

3) Elevating Team Productivity in the Face of Challenges

Educational leaders frequently run into the rough waters of poor team productivity in their pursuit of excellence. The requirement needed to address this issue is a diverse strategy that focuses on the specific dynamics of the educational environment.

Turbulence Point 3: Overcoming Low Team Productivity

Poor team productivity can be caused by a number of things, including a lack of drive, unclear expectations, and poor communication.

Productivity-Enhancing Strategies:

a) *Goal Clarity*: Ensure that each team member is aware of their own responsibilities and the team's overall goals. Clarity removes uncertainty and gives people the ability to work with purpose.

b) *Skill Development*: Invest in chances for professional growth that are specific to the requirements of the team. Giving team members the necessary information and skills improves their capacity to contribute successfully.

c) *Feedback Loop*: Create an ongoing feedback loop in which constructive criticism is freely given and received. A culture of growth and improvement is fostered via frequent feedback sessions.

d) *Honoring Milestones*: Honor and recognize both minor and major milestones. Progress is celebrated because it gives people a sense of success and it's motivational.

Examples and Details

- *Create a Culture of Collaboration*: Districts can create a culture of collaboration by emphasizing the importance of teamwork in all aspects of school life. This can be done through classroom activities, professional development opportunities, and school-wide celebrations of teamwork. For example, a school could implement a collaborative learning program where students work together in small groups on projects and assignments. The school could also offer professional development workshops on teamwork and collaboration strategies for teachers. Additionally, the school could hold a "Teamwork Week" to celebrate the importance of teamwork and to recognize the contributions of successful teams.

- *Value Diversity*: Districts can value diversity by creating an inclusive environment where all students feel welcome and respected. This can be done by celebrating different cultures and perspectives as well as providing opportunities for students to learn from each other.

In order to realize our goal of a vibrant educational environment, it is critical for us as educational leaders and school principals to be able to negotiate the uncertainty surrounding team formation. We not only survive the storm, but also come out stronger and more resilient by leveraging the power of relationships, encouraging a collaborative attitude, and boosting team productivity. Our unshakable commitment to efficient teamwork will guide us toward calmer waters and broader horizons in the constantly evolving educational scene.

CHAPTER 7

Similar to everyday life, we frequently encounter turmoil on our educational journeys; these are the times of doubt, difficulty, and change that can either derail us or help us advance. We have reached a turning point in our investigation of "The CPR of Navigating Educational Turbulence," where we go deeply into the core of the issue. The profound Cost, Price, and Benefits of sailing through the storms of scholastic turmoil will be revealed in this final chapter.

Cost of Turbulence

There is a cost associated with the experience of turbulence in education. While it definitely costs money and resources, there is an emotional and psychological toll that is frequently factored in as well. I have personally experienced the magnitude of these expenditures as a leader in education. The teachers and kids tend to suffer the most when a school faces unforeseen difficulties. The emotional cost can be heavy—from the restless hours spent thinking about answers to the weight of obligation we feel.

The disruption it causes to the flow of learning is one of the main drawbacks of educational turbulence. Both educators and students flourish in predictable settings with established routines and a general feeling of safety and predictability. When this delicate balance is upset, it makes pupils uneasy and causes teachers to scramble to modify their lesson plans. The human cost in this situation cannot be overstated; stress levels increase, morale plummets and burnout poses a serious danger.

Price of Turbulence

Beyond the short-term difficulties, there are larger costs associated with handling educational turbulence. Missed opportunities, a shift of focus, and a realignment of priorities are some examples of how it shows up. Financially, schools might find themselves allocating more funds to crisis management than to enhancing learning opportunities. The price is then paid in the form of strained relationships that have developed between the school community and outside parties.

Educational Turbulence also has the ability to undermine trust. Any effective educational institution is built on trust, therefore when trouble arises, parents, students, and staff may have doubts about the institution's ability to stay afloat. Building trust requires time and deliberate work, which detracts from the main objective of promoting learning and development.

Rewards of Navigating Turbulence

Managing educational turbulence offers immeasurable advantages, despite the challenges and costs. Although they might not always be perceptible at first, these advantages serve as the cornerstone of our educational path.

Resilience and flexibility: These are the qualities that go beyond the classroom and are essential for success in the real world. Anything involving turbulence forces us to develop these abilities. Pupils discover that setbacks are not barriers to advancement, but rather stepping stones. When faced with challenges, educators emerge as leaders who create innovative methods to engage kids.

Community Strengthening: Adversity has a unique ability to unite people. When there is a crisis, the school community comes together, forging a bond and a common goal. Collaboration between parents, teachers, students, and administration fosters a sense of unity that goes far beyond the turmoil itself.

Progress and Innovation: Managing educational turbulence compels us to question the status quo and look for novel solutions. Schools that accept change grow stronger and become better equipped to deliver a top-notch education. Educational leaders adopt technology, cutting-edge teaching techniques, and interdisciplinary strategies that enhance the learning process because they recognize the need to adapt.

Real-life Lessons: The lessons that navigating turbulence in educational leadership teaches are perhaps its most significant reward. The importance of persistence, empathy, and problem-solving is demonstrated to students personally. These lessons influence students' character and equip them to deal with future uncertainty outside of the classroom.

Conclusion

The complex interaction between cost, price, and benefits in the field of education is encapsulated by the Idea of managing educational turbulence. Although the cost and price of this instability should not be underestimated, the ultimate result of these difficulties have the power to change people, communities, and entire educational institutions. Let us keep in mind as we look back on this journey, that educational turbulence is not a sign of failure but a chance for growth while focusing on what is important to education and leaders. We learn to navigate through storms, and it is through these experiences that we grow stronger, wiser, and more tenacious. Let's accept turbulence and its intent-- as a necessary component of our educational journey, because it holds the promise of positively impacting all our scholars as we encounter them each and every day.